Killer Technique®: Bass Guitar

by Collin Bay

1 2

Visit us on the Web at www.melbay.com — E-mail us at email@melbay.com

Table of Contents

Introduction

Killer Technique: Bass Guitar is a technique and daily study book inspired by Corey Christiansen's *Gig Savers: Killer Technique* book for guitar (MB# 20028). This book provides concepts and daily routines to help players gain facility on their instrument by improving technique and avoiding injury. It is useful for musicians of any level. This book will work for any variety of bass guitar—electric, acoustic, or fretless. The exercises can also be easily adapted to fit a five- or six-string bass.

These exercises, like any exercises, should be tackled slowly at first; tempo can gradually be increased over time. This will ensure proper technique is employed from the beginning, thus avoiding injury. They can be used as a warm-up or as full-speed technical studies.

Many of the exercises focus on one hand or the other; others are designed specifically to improve synchronicity between the two hands. Musicians can also use these exercises as the genesis for new exercises they can develop themselves.

This book will be presented in string numbers, fret numbers and fretboard diagrams rather than standard notation or tab. Practicing with a metronome is recommended.

Left-Hand Workout

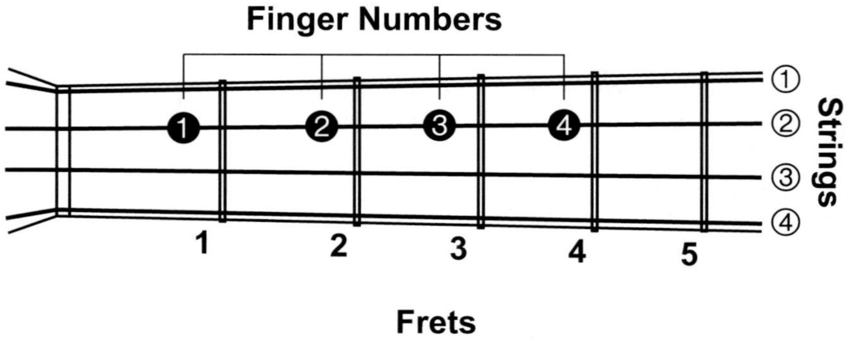

Index Middle

		i	*m*	*i*	*m*
Fret	–	1	2	3	4
String	–	2	2	2	2

In the first exercise, play the pattern up and down all four strings without reversing the pattern's direction. Give each note the same time value; the rhythm will be steady, equal for every note. If practicing with a metronome, each note can get a beat, a half a beat, or a quarter of a beat. Make sure you can play each exercise flawlessly before increasing the tempo. Begin by trying the exercise in first position; after you feel comfortable there, try moving the exercise up the neck—you can also move the pattern up one fret each time it is played through all four strings. Do the entire exercise with one finger on your right hand; then try another finger.

	i i i i	*i i i i*	*i i i i*	*i i i i*
*Fret:	1-2-3-4	1-2-3-4	1-2-3-4	1-2-3-4
String:	1-1-1-1	2-2-2-2	3-3-3-3	4-4-4-4

Reverse String Order

	i i i i	*i i i i*	*i i i i*	*i i i i*
*Fret:	1-2-3-4	1-2-3-4	1-2-3-4	1-2-3-4
String:	4-4-4-4	3-3-3-3	2-2-2-2	1-1-1-1

*Because this exercise is shown in first position, the fret number also corresponds to the left-hand finger number.

The next variation of this exercise addresses synchronization between the two hands. Try picking each note two or four times, alternating picking between the index and middle fingers on your right hand. Once you feel comfortable, return to picking each note once.

	i m i m	*i m i m*	*i m i m*	*i m i m*	
Fret:	1-1-1-1	2-2-2-2	3-3-3-3	4-4-4-4	Repeat Down and Up All Four Strings
String:	1-1-1-1	1-1-1-1	1-1-1-1	1-1-1-1	

	i m	*i m*	*i m*	*i m*	
Fret:	1-1	2-2	3-3	4-4	Repeat Down and Up All Four Strings
String:	1-1	1-1	1-1	1-1	

	i m i m	
Fret:	1-2-3-4	Repeat Down and Up All Four Strings
String:	1-1-1-1	

Make sure each note is clear; avoid any muffled, "flubbed" notes. Also strive for rhythmic accuracy. If a pause or unclear note is heard, isolate the two fingers that are not linking up and practice them separately. Many people, for example, have a difficult time playing smoothly between the third and fourth finger. To address this problem, use a more specific, small pattern, such as the following.

Fret:	3-4	3-4	3-4	3-4	Repeat Down and Up All Four Strings
String:	1-1	1-1	1-1	1-1	

All of the permutations of 1-2-3-4 are presented below. Any combination can be used in this exercise. It is recommended to focus on mastering one or two sets at a time.

1-2-3-4	2-1-3-4	3-1-2-4	4-1-2-3
1-2-4-3	2-1-4-3	3-1-4-2	4-1-3-2
1-3-2-4	2-3-1-4	3-2-1-4	4-2-1-3
1-3-4-2	2-3-4-1	3-2-4-1	4-2-3-1
1-4-2-3	2-4-1-3	3-4-1-2	4-3-1-2
1-4-3-2	2-4-3-1	3-4-2-1	4-3-2-1

Presented below is a typical workout, using pattern 1-2-3-4 as an example. Repeat the pattern through strings 1-4; then move up a fret and continue with strings 4-1. Reverse the direction when the fourth finger reaches the twelfth fret.

Strings 1-4. Pattern:1-2-3-4 (any pattern can be used)

Pos. I

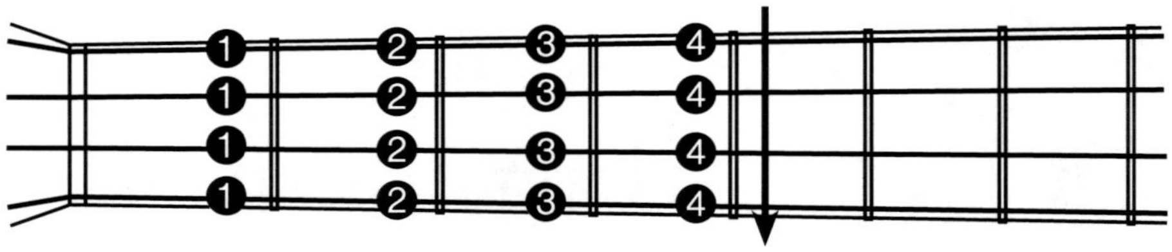

Strings 4-1

Pos. II

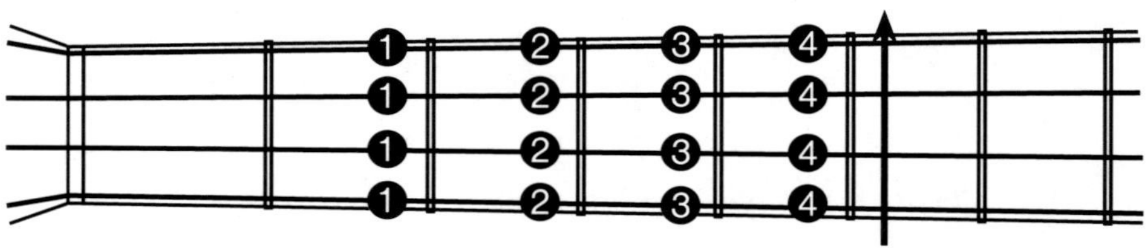

Strings 1-4, etc. Reverse when the 4th finger reaches the twelfth fret.

Pos. III

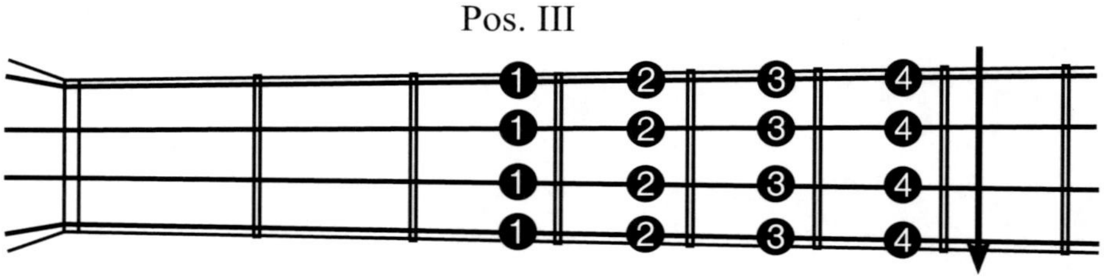

Right-Hand Workout

I used to study guitar with John Scofield. He once told me that just about anyone can develop excellent left-hand technique; what really sets guitarists apart, he said—and this is true of bass guitarists as well—is right-hand technique.

The following exercises use only open strings in the beginning. As with the other exercises, play the patterns from the fourth string to the first, then reverse the direction. We'll focus on using both the index ("*i*") and middle ("*m*") fingers and start with adjacent strings.

①

	i m i m	*i m i m*	*i m i m*	*i m i m*	*i m i m*	*i m i m*
Fret:	0-0-0-0	0-0-0-0	0-0-0-0	0-0-0-0	0-0-0-0	0-0-0-0
String:	2-1-2-1	2-1-2-1	3-2-3-2	3-2-3-2	4-3-4-3	4-3-4-3

②

	i m i m	*i m i m*	*i m i m*
Fret:	0-0-0-0	0-0-0-0	0-0-0-0
String:	2-1-2-1	3-2-3-2	4-3-4-3

③

	i m	*i m*	*i m*
Fret:	0-0	0-0	0-0
String:	2-1	3-2	4-3

④

	m i m i	*m i m i*	*m i m i*	*m i m i*	*m i m i*	*m i m i*
Fret:	0-0-0-0	0-0-0-0	0-0-0-0	0-0-0-0	0-0-0-0	0-0-0-0
String:	1-2-1-2	1-2-1-2	2-3-2-3	2-3-2-3	3-4-3-4	3-4-3-4

⑤

	m i m i	*m i m i*	*m i m i*
Fret:	0-0-0-0	0-0-0-0	0-0-0-0
String:	1-2-1-2	2-3-2-3	3-4-3-4

⑥

	m i	*m i*	*m i*
Fret:	0-0	0-0	0-0
String:	1-2	2-3	3-4

Exercises 1-6 present numerical sequences in sets of eight, four and two notes. The following exercises will present fret and string combos—like exercises 1-6, they should be practiced in sets of eight, four and two notes.

⑦

	i m i m	*i m i m*	*i m i m*	*i m i m*
Fret:	0-0-0-0	0-0-0-0	0-0-0-0	0-0-0-0
String:	3-1-3-1	3-1-3-1	4-2-4-2	4-2-4-2

⑧

	i m i m	*i m i m*
Fret:	0-0-0-0	0-0-0-0
String:	3-1-3-1	4-2-4-2

⑨

	m i m i	*m i m i*	*m i m i*	*m i m i*
Fret:	0-0-0-0	0-0-0-0	0-0-0-0	0-0-0-0
String:	1-3-1-3	1-3-1-3	2-4-2-4	2-4-2-4

⑩

	m i m i	*m i m i*
Fret:	0-0-0-0	0-0-0-0
String:	1-3-1-3	2-4-2-4

⑪

	i m i m
Fret:	0-0-0-0
String:	4-1-4-1

⑫

	m i m i
Fret:	0-0-0-0
String:	1-4-1-4

13

	i m m i	i m m i	i m m i	i m m i	i m m i	i m m i
Fret:	0-0-0-0	0-0-0-0	0-0-0-0	0-0-0-0	0-0-0-0	0-0-0-0
String:	2-1-1-2	2-1-1-2	3-2-2-3	3-2-2-3	4-3-3-4	4-3-3-4

14

	i m m i	i m m i	i m m i
Fret:	0-0-0-0	0-0-0-0	0-0-0-0
String:	2-1-1-2	3-2-2-3	4-3-3-4

15

	m i i m	m i i m	m i i m	m i i m	m i i m	m i i m
Fret:	0-0-0-0	0-0-0-0	0-0-0-0	0-0-0-0	0-0-0-0	0-0-0-0
String:	1-2-2-1	1-2-2-1	2-3-3-2	2-3-3-2	3-4-4-3	3-4-4-3

16

	m i i m	m i i m	m i i m
Fret:	0-0-0-0	0-0-0-0	0-0-0-0
String:	1-2-2-1	2-3-3-2	3-4-4-3

17

	i m m i	i m m i	i m m i	i m m i
Fret:	0-0-0-0	0-0-0-0	0-0-0-0	0-0-0-0
String:	3-1-1-3	3-1-1-3	4-2-2-4	4-2-2-4

18

	i m m i	i m m i
Fret:	0-0-0-0	0-0-0-0
String:	3-1-1-3	4-2-2-4

	m i i m	m i i m
Fret:	0-0-0-0	0-0-0-0
String:	1-3-3-1	2-4-4-2

19

	m i i m	m i i m	m i i m	m i i m
Fret:	0-0-0-0	0-0-0-0	0-0-0-0	0-0-0-0
String:	1-3-3-1	1-3-3-1	2-4-4-2	2-4-4-2

20

	i m m i	i m m i
Fret:	0-0-0-0	0-0-0-0
String:	4-1-1-4	4-1-1-4

㉑

	i m m i
Fret:	0-0-0-0
String:	4-1-1-4

㉒

	m i i m	*m i i m*
Fret:	0-0-0-0	0-0-0-0
String:	1-4-4-1	1-4-4-1

㉓

	m i i m
Fret:	0-0-0-0
String:	1-4-4-1

Synchronizing Both Hands

Now we will combine the left-hand exercises with the exercises for the right hand. Examples below.

	m i m i	*m i m i*	*m i m i*
Fret:	2-3-4-1	2-3-4-1	2-3-4-1
String:	1-2-1-2	2-3-2-3	3-4-3-4

	i m i m	*i m i m*
Fret:	3-1-2-4	3-1-2-4
String:	3-1-3-1	4-2-4-2

	i m m i	*i m m i*	*i m m i*
Fret:	1-2-3-4	1-2-3-4	1-2-3-4
String:	2-1-1-2	3-2-2-3	4-3-3-4

	m i i m	*m i i m*
Fret:	1-4-2-3	1-4-2-3
String:	1-3-3-1	2-4-4-2

	m i i m	*m i i m*	*m i i m*
Fret:	1-3-2-4	1-3-2-4	1-3-2-4
String:	1-2-2-1	2-3-3-2	3-4-4-3

In the above examples, the fret number is the left-hand finger number, as the examples are shown in the first position; the fingerings will remain the same as the exercises are moved up the neck.

By combining every left-hand four-fingered combination (permutation) with every possible four-string combination, an enormous number of exercises can be formulated. The chart below shows the various string set combinations, of which there are 24. These string sets may then be combined with any of the left-hand fingerings presented in the first part of the book.

1	**2**	**3**	**4**	**Order of original set**
1234	**2134**	**3124**	**4123**	Set 1234 yields the following string groups
12**43**	21**43**	31**42**	41**32**	Last two digits are reversed
1**3**24	2**3**14	3**2**14	4**2**13	Second number is next highest–last two digits in order
13**42**	23**41**	32**41**	42**31**	Last two digits are reversed
1**4**23	2**4**13	3**4**12	4**3**12	Second number is next highest–last two digits in order
14**32**	24**31**	34**21**	43**21**	Last two digits are reversed

An example of how to combine a string grouping and a left-hand fingering is shown below.

Fret: 1-3-2-4 String: 1-2-3-4	(Move this pattern like the other patterns after its completion. Reverse the direction when the fourth finger reaches the 12th fret.)

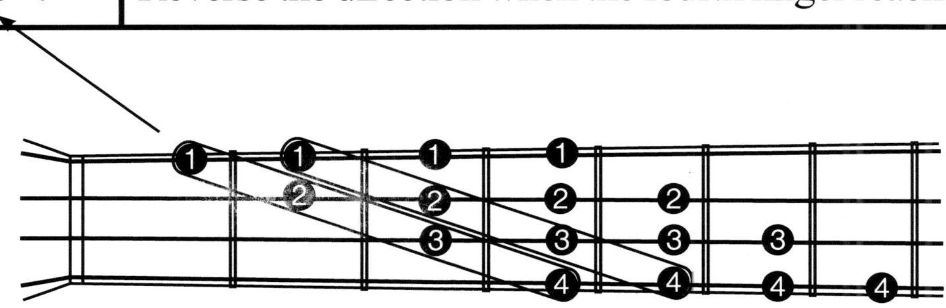

Mix the plethora of possible string groupings with the many left-hand fingering combinations; then, move each exercise up one fret after its completion.

All of the previous examples for the left-hand have worked the fingers while in a fixed position. Moving the patterns up or down one fret each time the pattern is completed is a good start at getting the left hand moving in a horizontal fashion, but doesn't really facilitate good linear motion. The following exercises should be repeated on all four strings even though they are shown on only one string. They will help with accuracy when moving up and down the neck.

First, select any note on the first string between frets five and ten. Then, play the same note with each of the four left-hand fingers. Play this exercise slowly at first. This is a good way to develop accuracy when the left hand has to move up and down the neck.

Fret:	7-7-7-7
Fingering:	1-2-3-4-etc.
String:	1-1-1-1

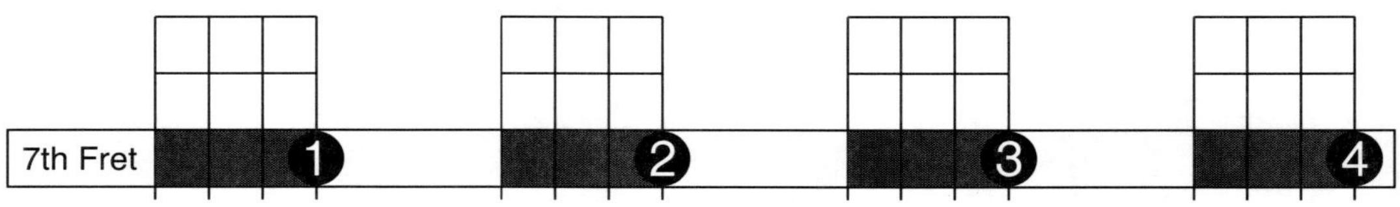

Here's another good linear movement workout. Notice the notes played on the bass move down and up the neck while the left-hand fingering moves in the opposite direction. Remember to play these exercises on all four strings.

Fret:	7-6-5-4-5-6-7
Fingering:	1-2-3-4-3-2-1
String:	1-1-1-1-1-1-1

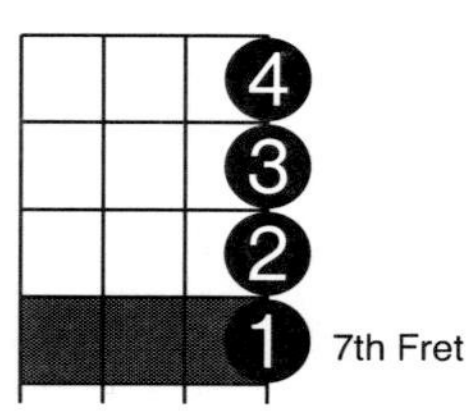

Notice the notes played on the instrument move down and up the neck while the left-hand fingering moves in the opposite direction. Play this exercise on all four strings.

Each of the four left-hand finger patterns can also be moved up and down the neck on one string. Make sure to play through the position shift seamlessly without skipping a beat or even pausing. Also be sure to reverse the direction of the left-hand movement.

Fret:	1-3-2-4-5-7-6-8-9-11-10-12
Fingering:	1-3-2-4-1-3-2-4-1- 3 - 2 - 4
String:	1-1-1-1-1-1-1-1-1- 1 - 1 - 1

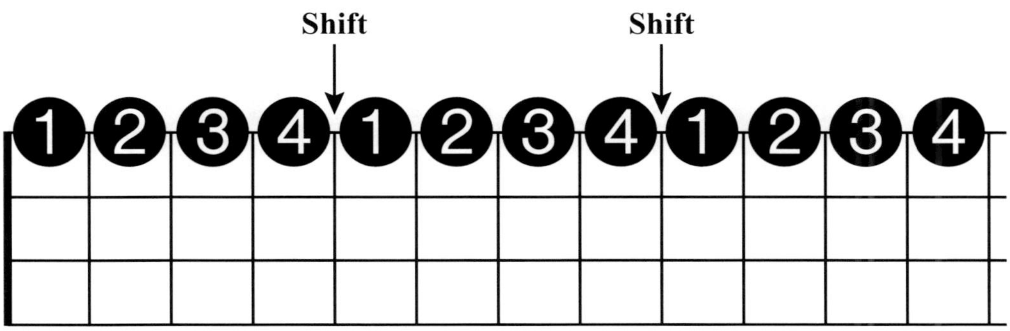

About the Author

Collin Bay began studying music as a four-year-old. He attended Interlochen Arts Academy and was part of the Interlochen Jazz Octet, recipient of Downbeat Magazine's top student award. He studied with Vijay Iyer and John Scofield at New School University in New York City. Fluent on many instruments and in many styles, he has performed on four continents both as a solo artist and as a member of various ensembles. He has shared the stage with MacArthur Fellows and has appeared on albums that have cracked the top-20 on iTunes world music chart. Having begun at Mel Bay editing books as a teen, Collin now works in Artist Relations and Product Development for the company. He resides in St. Louis and enjoys running with his dog. He is Mel Bay's youngest grandson.

Notes

MEL BAY®